EVERY YEAR

MW00955993

THE COMING OF WINTER

BRINGS ABOUT THE FREEZE

BUT ALSO CELEBRATIONS

LIGHTS DANCE IN THE SKY

BOUGHS OF HOLLY HANGING HIGH

UPON THE DOOR THERE HANGS A WREATH

FESTOONED WITH RIBBONS AND SILVER BELLS

THE GIFTS ARE READY, THE TREE AS WELL

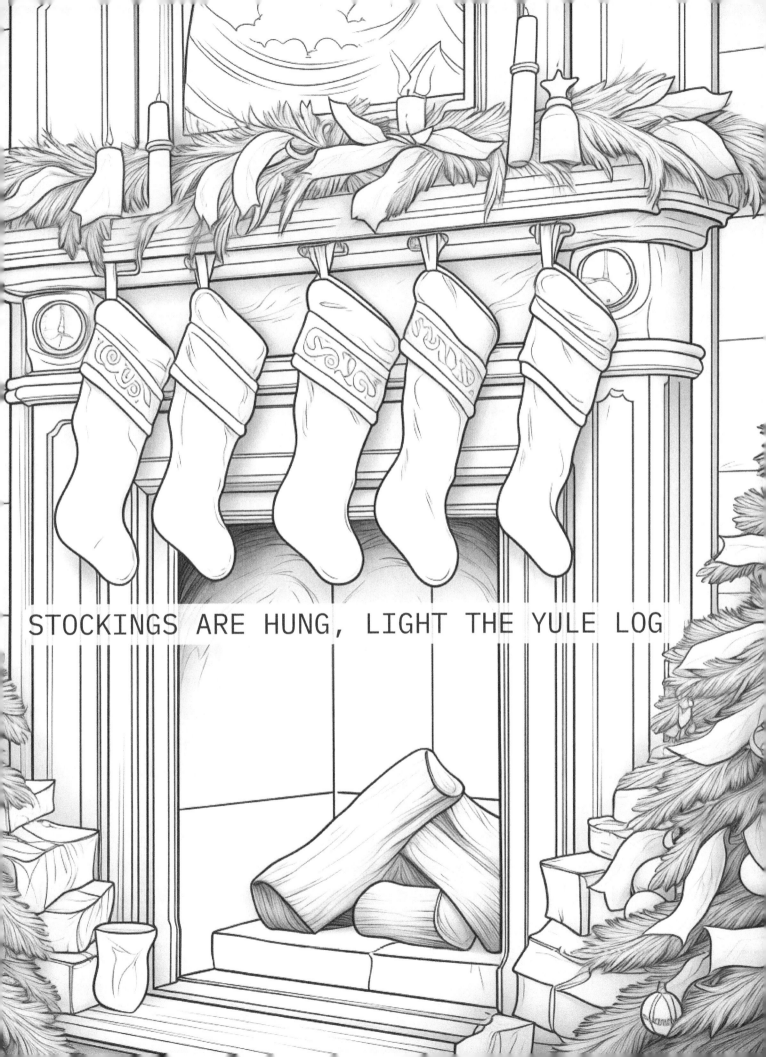

STOCKINGS ARE HUNG, LIGHT THE YULE LOG

STAY COZY INSIDE, AWAY FROM FREEZING FOG

HERE'S A JOLLY SNOWMAN

NATURE ITSELF PUTS ON A DISPLAY

MR. CRITTER IS OUT SHOPPING TODAY

TO TAKE HIS MIND OFF THE FACT THAT MRS. CRITTER WENT A LITTLE WILD WITH THE DECORATIONS.

MOM READS A STORY BEFORE IT'S TIME FOR BED

WHERE SUGAR PLUM
FAIRIES WILL DANCE
ON YOUR HEAD

RAMBUNCTIOUS CHILDREN HAVE A SNOWBALL FIGHT

THEY DON'T SAY "PLEASE" OR "THANK YOU"
OR EVEN "GOOD NIGHT"

BROKEN TOYS EVERWHERE STREWN

THEY VANDALIZE THEIR LOCKER ROOM

BROKEN WINDOWS DONE WITH SPITE

ABANDONED HOUSES SET ALIGHT

AND LET'S HAVE A MOMENT OF
SILENCE FOR THAT TIME THEY
RAZED THE CITY OF YAR-HABBATH
AND ENSLAVED THE PEACEFUL
UFHENSHI WHO INHABITED
THAT ONCE BEAUTIFUL PLACE.

FOR SUCH AS THEY, SANTA
WILL PAY NO VISIT ON
CHRISTMAS EVE

INSTEAD, KRAMPUS COMES!
THERE'LL BE NO REPRIEVE!

HE MAKES HIS WAY THROUGH VILLAGE STREETS

ENTERING HOMES

CLIMBING THROUGH DREAMS

HE LOADS THE WICKED INTO HIS SACK

AND WHERE HE TAKES THEM,
THEY NEVER COME BACK

SO REMEMBER WHY WE CELEBRATE
THIS VERY SPECIAL DAY

AND LISTEN TO EVERYTHING
YOUR PARENTS SAY

ALSO, WILL SOMEBODY PLEASE GET
GRANDMA AWAY FROM THE EGG NOG
THAT'S LIKE HER 8TH GLASS

Made in the USA
Monee, IL
02 December 2024

71473696R00046